Algorithmic Healing: Embracing AI for Better Mental Health

(Decode Your Mind, Design Your Life)

Krishna Dubey

Table of contents

Introduction

We are living in a time when machines can recognize our faces, understand our voices, and even finish our sentences. Technology is evolving fast — but so are our needs for emotional support, self-awareness, and healing. *Algorithmic Healing* was born out of this crossroads.

Mental health struggles are real, rising, and deeply personal. At the same time, artificial intelligence is no longer science fiction — it's quietly becoming part of our everyday lives. This book is not about replacing therapists or spiritual guides with machines. It's about reimagining how we can partner with technology to nurture our inner world more effectively, mindfully, and ethically.

But more importantly, you'll explore how to stay human in the process — to approach digital tools with discernment, integrity, and heart.

Whether you're someone navigating anxiety, a curious technophile, a wellness practitioner, or just wondering what role technology plays in your personal growth, this book is an invitation. An invitation to explore, to heal, and to embrace a future where compassion and code work together.

Welcome to a new way of healing.

Chapter 1:

Introduction to Algorithmic Healing

Understanding Mental Health in the Digital Age

Understanding mental health in the digital age requires an examination of how technology influences our well-being. In recent years, the proliferation of digital devices and platforms has transformed the way individuals access information, connect with others, and seek support for mental health issues. This shift brings both opportunities and challenges. On one hand, the internet provides a wealth of resources and forums where individuals can share experiences and find community support. On the other hand, the constant connectivity and exposure to social media can lead to increased anxiety, depression, and feelings of inadequacy.

The rise of AI-driven mental health solutions represents a significant advancement in how we approach mental wellness. These technologies utilize algorithms to analyze user behaviors, preferences, and emotional states, providing personalized recommendations and interventions. For instance, chatbots and virtual therapists can offer immediate assistance, making mental health resources more accessible to individuals who may hesitate to reach out for traditional therapy. This increased accessibility can lead to early intervention and help reduce the stigma associated with seeking help.

Despite the benefits, it is essential to consider the ethical implications of relying on algorithms for mental health support. Data privacy and security are paramount, as sensitive information can be vulnerable to breaches. Additionally, algorithmic biases can perpetuate stereotypes or fail to account for the diverse experiences of users. Ensuring that AI-driven solutions are inclusive and equitable is crucial for fostering trust and effectiveness. Mental health practitioners and technologists must collaborate to create systems that respect user autonomy while delivering accurate and helpful interventions.

Moreover, the impact of digital media consumption on mental health cannot be overlooked. While social media can facilitate connections, it can also contribute to feelings of isolation and inadequacy when users compare their lives to curated online personas. The phenomenon of "doomscrolling," or continuously consuming negative news, can exacerbate anxiety and stress. Understanding these dynamics is vital for individuals to navigate their digital environments mindfully. Encouraging practices such as digital detoxes and promoting positive online interactions can mitigate some of these adverse effects.

In sum, understanding mental health in the digital age involves recognizing the dual nature of technology as both a tool for support and a potential source of distress. By embracing AI-driven solutions and fostering a critical awareness of digital consumption, individuals can better navigate their mental health journeys. As technology continues to evolve, ongoing dialogue about its implications for mental well-being will be essential in shaping a future where mental health care is both innovative and compassionate.

The Rise of Artificial Intelligence

The rise of artificial intelligence (AI) marks a transformative era in numerous fields, including healthcare and mental health. This technological revolution is characterized by the development of algorithms that can analyze vast amounts of data, learn from patterns, and make predictions or decisions with minimal human intervention. In the realm of mental health, AI has begun to play a crucial role, offering innovative solutions that can enhance traditional therapeutic practices. As society grapples with increasing mental health challenges, the integration of AI into these solutions has the potential to revolutionize how individuals access care and manage their mental well-being.

One of the most significant advancements in AI relevant to mental health is the algorithmic personalization of treatment. By analyzing individual patient data, AI systems can identify specific patterns related to mental health conditions, allowing for tailored treatment plans. This personalized approach contrasts sharply with the one-size-fits-all methods of the past, where treatments were often generalized. With AI, mental health professionals can leverage detailed insights to curate interventions that align more closely with each patient's unique circumstances, preferences, and responses to previous treatments.

Moreover, AI-driven mental health solutions have expanded access to care in unprecedented ways. With the proliferation of mobile applications and online platforms, individuals can now engage with mental health resources from the comfort of their homes. AI chatbots and virtual therapists provide immediate support, helping users manage symptoms and offering coping strategies in real time. This accessibility is particularly beneficial for those living in remote areas or those who may hesitate to seek traditional therapy due to stigma or financial barriers. The ability to receive assistance at any time fosters a proactive approach to mental health management.

Additionally, AI's capacity for data analysis enables the identification of trends and risk factors at a population level. By aggregating data from diverse sources, researchers can gain insights into mental health issues that may be overlooked in smaller datasets. This broader understanding can inform public health initiatives and contribute to more effective prevention strategies. For example, AI can help identify emerging mental health crises within specific demographics, prompting timely interventions and resource allocation. This predictive capability signifies a shift toward a more anticipatory approach in mental health care.

However, as we embrace the rise of artificial intelligence in mental health, it is essential to address the ethical considerations and potential challenges that accompany such advancements. Issues such as data privacy, algorithmic bias, and the need for human oversight must be carefully navigated to ensure that AI serves as a complement to human care rather than a replacement. As we continue to explore the intersection of technology and mental health, fostering a collaborative environment where AI and mental health professionals work together will be crucial in maximizing the benefits while minimizing the risks. The future of mental health care lies in this balanced integration, where the unique strengths of AI enhance the healing process.

The Intersection of AI and Mental Health

The intersection of artificial intelligence (AI) and mental health represents a transformative frontier in healthcare, where technology and compassion converge to enhance well-being. As mental health challenges proliferate globally, the demand for effective and accessible solutions has never been more critical. AI-driven mental health solutions are emerging as powerful tools that can augment traditional therapeutic practices, providing innovative approaches to diagnosis, treatment, and ongoing support. By harnessing vast datasets and sophisticated algorithms, these technologies offer the potential to personalize care, ensuring that interventions are tailored to individual needs.

One of the most significant contributions of AI in mental health is its capability to analyze patient data and identify patterns that may not be immediately apparent to clinicians. Machine learning algorithms can process vast amounts of information, including clinical notes, social media activity, and even biometric data, to uncover insights regarding a patient's mental health status. This data-driven approach allows for early detection of mental health issues, enabling timely interventions that can alter the course of a condition. By integrating AI into routine assessments, health professionals can enhance their diagnostic accuracy and empower patients with a clearer understanding of their mental health landscape.

AI also facilitates the development of personalized treatment plans. Algorithms can recommend interventions based on a patient's unique profile, preferences, and historical responses to various treatments. This personalization is crucial, as mental health is not a one-size-fits-all domain. By considering individual differences in genetics, environment, and personal history, AI-driven solutions can optimize treatment strategies, increasing the likelihood of successful outcomes. Moreover, ongoing monitoring through AI can help adjust these plans in real-time, ensuring that patients receive the most effective care throughout their healing journey.

In addition to enhancing clinical practices, AI technologies provide new avenues for mental health support outside traditional settings. Mobile applications powered by AI can offer 24/7 access to mental health resources, including chatbots that provide immediate support and guidance. These tools can address issues such as anxiety or depression, allowing users to engage in self-care practices when they need it most. Furthermore, AI can facilitate peer support networks by connecting individuals with similar experiences, fostering a sense of community and reducing feelings of isolation. This democratization of mental health care ensures that help is available to a broader audience, regardless of geographical or financial barriers.

While the potential benefits of AI in mental health are significant, ethical considerations must guide its implementation. Issues such as data privacy, algorithmic bias, and the need for human oversight are paramount in developing AI solutions that are both effective and trustworthy. As we embrace algorithmic healing, it is essential to prioritize transparency, accountability, and inclusivity in the design of AI-driven mental health interventions. By doing so, we can create an ecosystem where technology serves as a valuable ally in the pursuit of mental well-being, promoting a future where everyone has access to the support they need.

Chapter 2:

The Algorithm of You

Personal Data and Mental Health

The intersection of personal data and mental health is increasingly significant in today's digital age. Individuals generate vast amounts of data through their online activities, interactions, and even through wearables that monitor physical and emotional states. This data can illuminate patterns in behavior, mood fluctuations, and stress triggers, thereby offering insights that were previously difficult to quantify. By harnessing personal data, AI-driven mental health solutions can create a more personalized approach to mental health care, tailoring interventions and support systems to meet individual needs.

One of the primary advantages of utilizing personal data in mental health is the ability to track changes over time. With continuous monitoring and data collection, individuals can gain a better understanding of their mental health journey. This process allows for the identification of warning signs before they escalate into more significant issues. For example, a person may notice that their mood dips following certain activities or social interactions. By recognizing these patterns, they can make informed decisions about their lifestyle and seek appropriate interventions early.

However, the use of personal data in mental health raises important ethical considerations. Privacy and consent are paramount when dealing with sensitive information. Individuals must be fully informed about how their data will be used, stored, and protected. Moreover, the algorithms that analyze this data must be transparent and free from bias to ensure fair treatment across diverse populations. Educating users about their rights and the implications of data sharing is essential in fostering trust between individuals and mental health technologies.

AI-driven mental health solutions can also leverage personal data to enhance therapeutic practices. For instance, chatbots and virtual therapists can utilize data to provide real-time feedback and support based on the user's emotional state. This immediate responsiveness can help bridge gaps in traditional therapy, where individuals may only see a therapist once a week or month. By integrating personal data into these interactions, AI can help maintain a continuous support system that adapts to the evolving needs of the user.

Ultimately, the integration of personal data into mental health solutions represents a transformative shift in how care is delivered. By embracing AI technology, individuals can access tailored support that resonates with their unique experiences. As mental health continues to gain recognition as a critical component of overall well-being, the responsible use of personal data will be instrumental in developing effective, personalized treatments. This evolution calls for a collaborative effort among technologists, mental health professionals, and users to ensure that the potential of AI is harnessed ethically and effectively.

How Algorithms Understand Behavior

Algorithms understand behavior through a combination of data analysis, pattern recognition, and predictive modeling. At their core, algorithms are designed to process vast amounts of information quickly, identifying trends and correlations that might not be immediately apparent to human observers. By collecting data from various sources, such as social media interactions, wearable health devices, and self-reported questionnaires, algorithms can create a nuanced profile of an individual's mental health status and behavioral patterns. This data-driven approach allows algorithms to discern not only current states of well-being but also potential risks and triggers for mental health issues.

One fundamental aspect of how algorithms understand behavior is through machine learning. Machine learning models are trained on historical data to recognize patterns and make predictions. For instance, an algorithm might analyze past interactions of individuals who experienced anxiety and identify common factors such as sleep patterns, social interactions, or life events. By continuously learning from new data inputs, these algorithms can refine their understanding and improve their predictive accuracy, resulting in more personalized mental health interventions tailored to the individual user.

Algorithms also utilize natural language processing (NLP) to interpret and analyze human language, which can provide significant insights into mental health. By analyzing text from social media posts, chat logs, or journal entries, algorithms can detect emotional tone, sentiment, and even specific mental health concerns. This capability allows for the identification of individuals who may be experiencing distress or are at risk of developing more serious mental health conditions. By leveraging NLP, AI-driven solutions can offer timely support and resources based on the individual's expressed needs and emotional state.

Moreover, the integration of behavioral data with traditional mental health assessments enhances the effectiveness of AI-driven mental health solutions. Algorithms can cross-reference behavioral indicators with clinical data to create a comprehensive picture of an individual's mental health. For example, by combining data from therapy sessions with real-time behavioral inputs, algorithms can help clinicians track progress and adjust treatment plans dynamically. This holistic approach can lead to improved outcomes, as interventions can be more accurately aligned with the patient's evolving needs.

Finally, ethical considerations play a crucial role in how algorithms understand behavior and their application in mental health. Transparency in data usage, informed consent, and privacy protection are essential elements that ensure user trust and safety. As algorithms become more sophisticated, it is imperative for developers to prioritize ethical standards and engage with mental health professionals to create solutions that respect individual autonomy while effectively addressing mental health challenges. By fostering a responsible framework for algorithmic understanding of behavior, we can harness the power of AI to promote better mental health outcomes for all.

The Role of Personalization in Mental Wellness

Personalization in mental wellness refers to the tailored approaches that address the unique needs and preferences of individuals. In the context of mental health, this means recognizing that each person's experiences, symptoms, and coping mechanisms differ significantly. Personalized mental wellness strategies can enhance engagement and effectiveness, fostering a deeper connection between individuals and their mental health journeys. The integration of personalization in therapeutic practices allows for more nuanced responses to the complexities of mental health issues, catering to diverse populations and varying life experiences.

Artificial intelligence plays a pivotal role in facilitating personalization in mental wellness. By analyzing vast amounts of data, AI-driven solutions can identify patterns and correlations that might otherwise go unnoticed. These insights enable healthcare providers to create customized treatment plans that reflect an individual's specific circumstances, preferences, and historical responses to various interventions. For example, AI algorithms can assess an individual's responses to different therapeutic modalities and recommend the most effective ones, thereby improving outcomes and minimizing trial-and-error approaches that can be frustrating for patients.

Moreover, the incorporation of personalization in mental health solutions enhances user experience and satisfaction. When individuals receive tailored recommendations, they are more likely to engage with the interventions. For instance, digital platforms that utilize AI can adapt their content and delivery methods based on user interactions, ensuring that the support provided resonates with the individual. This adaptability not only fosters a sense of ownership over one's mental health journey but also encourages continuous participation, which is crucial for effective treatment and support.

Personalized mental wellness strategies also extend to preventative measures, allowing individuals to take proactive steps in managing their mental health. AI-driven tools can help identify early warning signs of mental distress by analyzing behavioral patterns and emotional responses. By intervening before a crisis occurs, these personalized approaches can significantly reduce the severity of mental health issues and promote resilience. This proactive stance is essential in creating a culture of mental wellness where individuals feel empowered to prioritize their mental health before challenges escalate.

In conclusion, personalization in mental wellness is essential for fostering effective and engaging mental health solutions. The role of AI in this personalization cannot be overstated; it provides the necessary data-driven insights to tailor interventions to the individual. By embracing these personalized strategies, we can enhance the effectiveness of mental health treatments, promote preventative measures, and ultimately contribute to a more holistic approach to mental wellness. As we continue to explore the intersection of technology and mental health, the potential for AI-driven personalization remains a promising frontier in the pursuit of improved mental well-being for all.

Chapter 3:

AI-Driven Mental Health Solutions

Overview of AI Applications in Mental Health

Artificial Intelligence (AI) has emerged as a transformative force in various sectors, and mental health is no exception. With the growing recognition of mental health issues and the need for accessible and effective solutions, AI applications are being integrated into therapeutic practices, diagnostics, and patient management. These innovative tools aim to enhance the understanding of mental health conditions, personalize treatment plans, and improve overall patient outcomes. By leveraging vast amounts of data and complex algorithms, AI can assist mental health professionals in their decision-making processes and enable individuals to take more proactive roles in their mental well-being.

AI-driven mental health solutions can be broadly categorized into several areas, including chatbots, predictive analytics, and virtual reality therapies. Chatbots, powered by natural language processing, offer immediate support and resources to individuals in distress. They can engage in conversations, provide coping strategies, and guide users through exercises designed to alleviate symptoms of anxiety and depression. Predictive analytics, on the other hand, utilizes data from various sources, such as electronic health records and social media activity, to identify individuals at risk of developing mental health issues. This proactive approach allows for early intervention and tailored prevention strategies.

Another exciting application of AI in mental health is the use of virtual reality (VR) environments for therapeutic purposes. VR therapy can simulate real-life scenarios that trigger anxiety or phobias, allowing individuals to confront their fears in a controlled setting. This immersive experience can lead to significant reductions in symptoms and promote desensitization. Moreover, AI algorithms can track progress and adapt the therapy based on individual responses, ensuring a personalized approach that aligns with each person's unique needs.

AI's role in mental health extends beyond treatment and intervention; it also encompasses research and data analysis. By employing machine learning techniques, researchers can analyze patterns and trends in mental health data on a scale that was previously unattainable. This can lead to new insights into the causes of mental health disorders, the effectiveness of various treatments, and the identification of potential biomarkers for conditions. Such advancements can ultimately inform clinical practices and contribute to the development of more effective therapies.

Despite the promising potential of AI applications in mental health, challenges remain. Issues surrounding data privacy, ethical considerations, and the importance of maintaining a human connection in therapy are critical to address. As AI continues to evolve, it is essential to balance technological advancements with the human element that is vital to mental health care. Embracing AI in mental health has the potential to revolutionize the field, but it must be approached thoughtfully to ensure that it complements and enhances traditional therapeutic practices rather than replacing them.

Chatbots and Virtual Therapists

Chatbots and virtual therapists represent a significant leap forward in the realm of mental health care, offering accessible and immediate support to individuals seeking help. These AI-driven tools leverage natural language processing and machine learning algorithms to engage users in conversation, providing a semblance of therapeutic interaction. Unlike traditional therapy, where human practitioners guide the process, chatbots can be available 24/7, enabling users to seek assistance at any hour without the barriers of scheduling or location.

The algorithms powering these virtual therapists are designed to recognize emotional cues and respond empathetically. They can analyze the user's input to identify patterns of distress and suggest coping mechanisms or resources tailored to individual needs. This personalization is a key feature, as it allows the chatbot to adapt its responses based on the user's emotional state and previous interactions, creating a more engaging and supportive experience. The technology behind these tools continuously evolves, incorporating user feedback to enhance their effectiveness and relevance.

Privacy and confidentiality are paramount in mental health care, and chatbots are engineered to address these concerns. Many users may feel more comfortable discussing sensitive issues with a non-human entity, alleviating fears of judgment or stigma associated with seeking help. The anonymity provided by chatbots can encourage individuals who might otherwise avoid traditional therapy to take the first step towards mental wellness. However, it is essential for users to be aware of the limitations of these tools, recognizing that they are not a replacement for professional therapy but rather a supplementary resource.

Despite their advantages, the effectiveness of chatbots and virtual therapists can vary. While some users find them beneficial for managing anxiety, stress, or depression, others may require the nuanced understanding and empathy that only a human therapist can provide. Researchers are exploring how to enhance the capabilities of these AI-driven solutions, including integrating them with human oversight. This hybrid approach aims to combine the strengths of both human and machine, ensuring that users receive comprehensive support tailored to their unique circumstances.

The future of mental health care may see a greater integration of chatbots and virtual therapists alongside traditional methods. As technology advances, these AI tools will likely become more sophisticated, utilizing data analytics to predict user needs and outcomes. The potential for widespread accessibility and cost-effectiveness makes them an attractive option for improving mental health services globally. Embracing these innovations can pave the way for a more inclusive approach to mental wellness, empowering individuals to take control of their mental health journeys and seek help when they need it.

Predictive Analytics for Mental Health

Predictive analytics has emerged as a transformative tool in the field of mental health, enabling practitioners to anticipate and address potential issues before they escalate. By leveraging vast amounts of data collected from various sources, including electronic health records, social media interactions, and wearable technologies, predictive analytics can identify patterns and risk factors associated with mental health conditions. This proactive approach not only improves patient outcomes but also enhances the overall efficacy of mental health interventions, allowing for timely and tailored support.

One of the key components of predictive analytics is its ability to analyze historical data to forecast future trends. In mental health care, this means identifying individuals who may be at higher risk for developing conditions such as depression, anxiety, or substance abuse disorders. Machine learning algorithms can process complex datasets to discern subtle correlations that might be overlooked in traditional clinical assessments. As a result, mental health professionals can focus their resources on high-risk individuals, potentially preventing the onset of more severe symptoms and reducing the overall burden on healthcare systems.

Moreover, predictive analytics can enhance personalized treatment plans by integrating data-driven insights into therapeutic approaches. For instance, algorithms can assess a patient's unique characteristics, including their genetic makeup, lifestyle choices, and social environments, to recommend tailored interventions. This level of personalization not only increases the likelihood of successful treatment outcomes but also empowers patients by involving them in their care decisions. As mental health treatment evolves, the integration of predictive analytics presents a compelling opportunity to move beyond a one-size-fits-all model.

The ethical considerations surrounding predictive analytics in mental health are paramount. While the benefits are significant, the potential for misuse of data raises concerns about privacy, consent, and the risk of stigmatization. Therefore, it is crucial for practitioners and technologists to implement robust ethical guidelines that prioritize patient confidentiality and informed consent. Engaging patients in discussions about the use of their data can foster trust and ensure that predictive analytics serves to enhance their mental health journey rather than infringe upon their rights.

In conclusion, predictive analytics holds the promise of revolutionizing mental health care by offering insights that can lead to early intervention and personalized treatment options. As mental health professionals increasingly adopt these advanced analytics tools, ongoing collaboration between data scientists, clinicians, and patients will be essential. Together, they can navigate the complexities of mental health care, ensuring that predictive analytics not only serves as a powerful ally in treatment but also upholds the ethical standards necessary for fostering a compassionate and effective mental health system.

Chapter 4:

Benefits of **AI** in Mental Health Care

Accessibility and Affordability

Accessibility and affordability are critical considerations in the landscape of mental health care, especially as artificial intelligence (AI) continues to reshape the sector. Traditional mental health services often come with significant barriers, including geographical limitations, high costs, and a lack of qualified professionals. These limitations disproportionately affect marginalized communities and individuals with lower socioeconomic status. By integrating AI-driven solutions into mental health care, we can begin to dismantle these barriers, creating a more inclusive and equitable system that serves a broader demographic.

AI has the potential to enhance accessibility in several ways. Virtual therapy platforms powered by AI can provide round-the-clock support to individuals in remote or underserved areas. These platforms can use algorithms to match users with appropriate resources and tools, such as chatbots that offer immediate assistance or virtual therapists that can conduct sessions via video calls. This technology enables individuals to seek help without the constraints of location, thereby increasing the likelihood that they will access the mental health resources they need. Moreover, AI can help identify trends in mental health needs, allowing organizations to allocate resources more effectively where they are most needed.

Affordability remains a significant hurdle in mental health care access. Traditional therapeutic models often involve high fees, which can deter individuals from seeking help. AI-driven solutions have the potential to reduce costs significantly by automating certain aspects of care, such as initial assessments and routine check-ins. For example, AI can analyze user data to provide insights into mental health trends, allowing therapists to focus on more complex cases while routine maintenance is handled through automated means. This not only lowers costs but also frees up valuable time for mental health professionals to engage more deeply with clients who require specialized care.

In addition to cost reduction, AI can facilitate the development of low-cost, scalable mental health interventions. Apps and online platforms that utilize AI can offer self-guided resources, such as cognitive behavioral therapy (CBT) exercises, at little to no cost. These tools can empower individuals to take charge of their mental health, providing them with strategies to cope with stress, anxiety, and depression without the financial burden of traditional therapy. As these resources become more widely available, the overall stigma associated with seeking mental health care may diminish, encouraging a culture of openness and support.

Ultimately, the intersection of accessibility and affordability in AI-driven mental health solutions holds the promise of a transformative shift in how we approach mental health care. By leveraging technology, we can create an ecosystem that not only meets the diverse needs of individuals but also promotes a more sustainable model of care. As we embrace these innovations, it is essential to remain vigilant in ensuring that the benefits are distributed equitably, allowing everyone, regardless of their background or financial situation, to access the mental health support they deserve.

Reducing Stigma through Technology

Reducing stigma surrounding mental health has long been a challenge, but advancements in technology, particularly artificial intelligence, offer promising avenues for change. AI-driven mental health solutions can facilitate more open conversations about mental health, encouraging individuals to seek help without fear of judgment. By harnessing the power of data and algorithms, these tools can provide personalized, accessible support, helping to normalize mental health struggles as part of the human experience.

One significant way technology reduces stigma is through anonymity and privacy. Many AI-driven platforms allow users to engage with mental health resources without revealing their identities. This confidentiality can empower individuals to explore their mental health concerns and seek assistance without the fear of being labeled or judged by others. By providing a safe space for exploration, technology helps demystify mental health issues and fosters a culture of understanding and acceptance.

Moreover, social media platforms and mental health apps utilize algorithms to promote positive mental health narratives. By curating content that highlights personal stories of recovery and resilience, technology can shift public perception and create a more supportive environment. These platforms often feature user-generated content that resonates with a diverse audience, allowing individuals to share their experiences and connect with others facing similar challenges. This sense of community can help combat isolation and encourage more people to speak openly about their mental health journeys.

Educational tools powered by AI can also play a crucial role in reducing stigma. Interactive applications and virtual assistants can provide users with information about mental health, coping strategies, and resources for professional help. By making mental health education more accessible, technology empowers individuals to become informed advocates for themselves and others. This increased awareness can dismantle misconceptions and stereotypes surrounding mental health, fostering a more compassionate society.

Finally, AI can analyze trends and patterns in mental health data, providing insights that can inform public health campaigns and policies. By understanding the broader societal impacts of mental health, stakeholders can address stigma at a systemic level. With the right data, initiatives can be tailored to target specific demographics, breaking down barriers to care and promoting mental wellness. As technology continues to evolve, its potential to reduce stigma and enhance the conversation around mental health will be an essential aspect of fostering a healthier, more inclusive society.

Enhancing Patient Engagement

Enhancing patient engagement is a crucial aspect of improving mental health outcomes through AI-driven solutions. With the integration of algorithmic tools in mental health care, the traditional one-size-fits-all approach is being replaced by more personalized strategies. By leveraging data, AI can analyze individual patient behaviors, preferences, and responses to treatment, enabling healthcare providers to tailor their approaches accordingly. This personalization not only fosters a stronger connection between patients and their treatment plans but also empowers individuals to take an active role in their own mental health journey.

One effective way to enhance patient engagement is through the implementation of interactive digital platforms. These platforms can offer educational resources, self-assessment tools, and community forums, allowing patients to access information and support at their convenience. By utilizing AI algorithms, these platforms can adapt content to meet the specific needs of each user, thus making the information more relevant and engaging. Moreover, these tools can facilitate ongoing communication between patients and healthcare providers, ensuring that patients feel supported and informed throughout their treatment.

AI-driven mental health solutions also have the potential to enhance engagement by providing real-time feedback and monitoring. Wearable devices and mobile applications can track mood patterns, sleep quality, and other relevant metrics, allowing patients to gain insights into their mental health status. This immediate feedback can prompt users to reflect on their behaviors and emotions, fostering a deeper understanding of their mental health. By encouraging self-reflection, patients are more likely to engage with their treatment plans and actively participate in their recovery process.

Furthermore, gamification strategies can significantly boost patient engagement in mental health care. By incorporating game-like elements into therapeutic interventions, such as rewards for completing tasks or challenges, patients may find the process more enjoyable and motivating. AI algorithms can analyze user engagement data to refine these gamified experiences, ensuring they are effective and aligned with the patient's therapeutic goals. This approach not only makes the treatment process more enjoyable but also increases adherence to prescribed therapies, ultimately leading to better mental health outcomes.

Lastly, fostering a collaborative environment between patients and providers is essential in enhancing engagement. AI can facilitate this collaboration by providing healthcare professionals with insights derived from patient data, enabling them to better understand their patients' needs and preferences. This collaborative approach, where patients feel heard and valued, can lead to stronger therapeutic alliances and improved trust. When patients feel that they are partners in their mental health care, they are more likely to engage actively in their treatment, leading to sustainable improvements in their well-being.

Chapter 5:

Challenges and Ethical Considerations

Data Privacy and Security

Data privacy and security are paramount concerns when integrating artificial intelligence into mental health solutions. As these technologies increasingly collect and analyze personal data to provide tailored support, the need to safeguard sensitive information becomes critical. Mental health data often includes deeply personal details, such as emotional states, therapy progress, and treatment histories. The ethical implications of handling such data must be considered, as breaches could lead to severe consequences for individuals, including stigma, discrimination, and loss of trust in mental health systems.

To ensure data privacy, developers of AI-driven mental health solutions must adopt robust data protection practices. This includes employing encryption techniques to safeguard data during transmission and storage. Encryption ensures that even if data is intercepted, it remains unreadable without the proper decryption keys. Furthermore, anonymization techniques can help in minimizing the risks associated with data exposure. By stripping personally identifiable information from datasets, developers can still derive valuable insights while protecting individual privacy.

Compliance with legal frameworks and regulations is another crucial aspect of data privacy within the realm of AI and mental health. Various regulations, such as the General Data Protection Regulation (GDPR) in Europe and the Health Insurance Portability and Accountability Act (HIPAA) in the United States, set stringent guidelines on how personal health information should be handled. Organizations developing AI-driven mental health solutions must ensure they are compliant with such laws, which not only protect individual rights but also foster a culture of accountability within the industry.

Moreover, transparency in data usage is essential for building trust with users. Individuals should be informed about what data is being collected, how it will be used, and who will have access to it. This transparency empowers users to make informed decisions about their participation in AI-driven mental health applications. Providing users with control over their data—such as the ability to opt-out or delete their information—can enhance their sense of security and promote a more ethical approach to technology.

Finally, ongoing education about data privacy and security is necessary for both developers and users. Continuous training for developers can help them stay updated on best practices and emerging threats in data handling. Similarly, educating users about the importance of data privacy in mental health contexts can encourage them to engage more actively with the technologies designed to support them. By fostering a collaborative approach to data privacy, the intersection of AI and mental health can be navigated more safely and effectively, ultimately leading to improved mental health outcomes for all.

Bias in AI Algorithms

Bias in AI algorithms is a critical issue that has significant implications for the development and implementation of AI-driven mental health solutions. Algorithms, by their nature, learn from data to make predictions and decisions. However, if the data used to train these algorithms is biased, the outcomes can perpetuate existing inequalities or even introduce new forms of discrimination. This is particularly concerning in the realm of mental health, where decisions made by AI can affect diagnosis, treatment recommendations, and overall patient care.

One of the primary sources of bias in AI algorithms stems from the datasets used in training these systems. If the data is not representative of the diverse populations that will ultimately use the technology, the algorithm may fail to account for variations in mental health symptoms, treatment responses, and social contexts. For instance, an AI model trained predominantly on data from one demographic group may overlook the unique mental health challenges faced by individuals from different backgrounds, leading to misdiagnosis or inappropriate treatment plans.

Moreover, the biases can be both overt and subtle. Overt bias occurs when explicit stereotypes or prejudices are reflected in the data. Subtle biases, on the other hand, can emerge from the way data is collected or labeled. For example, if mental health conditions are recorded based on specific cultural norms or behaviors, individuals who do not conform to these norms may be inaccurately assessed. This can lead to a situation where AI-driven solutions do not serve all populations equitably, exacerbating disparities in mental health care.

As we embrace AI technologies for better mental health, it is essential to implement strategies that mitigate bias. This includes rigorous testing of algorithms across diverse datasets to ensure they perform well for all demographic groups. Additionally, incorporating feedback from mental health professionals and patients can help identify potential biases and areas for improvement. By prioritizing inclusivity in the development of AI algorithms, we can create more effective and equitable mental health solutions.

Finally, addressing bias in AI algorithms is not solely a technical challenge; it also requires a commitment to ethical considerations within the field of AI. Stakeholders, including developers, researchers, and policymakers, must work together to establish guidelines that promote fairness and accountability. As we continue to explore the intersection of technology and mental health, fostering an environment that recognizes and actively combats bias will be crucial for the ethical advancement of AI-driven mental health solutions. This concerted effort will ultimately lead to more accurate, effective, and compassionate care for individuals seeking support.

The Human Touch in Therapy

The integration of technology in mental health care has undoubtedly transformed the landscape of therapeutic practices. However, amid the advancements brought forth by artificial intelligence, the human touch remains an irreplaceable component in therapy. This subchapter explores the significance of human connection in the therapeutic process and how it complements AI-driven solutions. Understanding the dynamics of human empathy, rapport, and emotional intelligence is crucial for both practitioners and clients as they navigate the evolving landscape of mental health care.

Human interaction in therapy fosters a sense of safety and trust, which can significantly enhance the therapeutic experience. The nuances of face-to-face communication, including non-verbal cues such as body language and tone of voice, play a vital role in establishing rapport between therapist and client. These elements contribute to a deeper understanding of each individual's emotional state, which AI may struggle to interpret fully. While AI can analyze data and identify patterns, it lacks the innate ability to respond intuitively to complex human emotions, making the therapist's presence invaluable in the healing journey.

Moreover, the therapeutic alliance built through human connection is essential for effective treatment outcomes. Research consistently shows that the quality of the relationship between therapist and client is a crucial predictor of success in therapy. When clients feel understood and validated by their therapists, they are more likely to engage fully in the therapeutic process. AI technologies can supplement this relationship by providing tools and resources, but they cannot replace the empathy and personalized attention that a human therapist offers. As such, the most effective treatment models will be those that integrate AI with traditional therapeutic practices.

Additionally, the human touch in therapy allows for the exploration of complex emotional experiences that often cannot be quantified. Human therapists can navigate the subtleties of grief, trauma, and anxiety, offering support that resonates on a personal level. This emotional depth is vital, as mental health challenges are often intertwined with personal narratives that require careful unpacking. AI may assist in tracking symptoms or suggesting interventions, but it is the therapist's ability to engage in meaningful conversations that truly facilitates healing. This highlights the importance of maintaining a balance between technology and human interaction in mental health care.

In conclusion, while AI-driven solutions have the potential to revolutionize mental health care, the human touch remains an essential element of therapy. The combination of technological advancements and human empathy can lead to more comprehensive and effective treatment outcomes. As we embrace the future of mental health care, it is critical to recognize the unique contributions of both AI and human practitioners. By fostering collaboration between these two domains, we can enhance the therapeutic experience and ensure that individuals receive the compassionate care they need on their path to healing.

Chapter 6:

Case Studies of **AI** in Action

Successful AI Mental Health Apps

The rise of technology has transformed various sectors, including mental health care. Successful AI mental health apps represent a significant advancement in providing accessible and effective support to individuals facing mental health challenges. These applications utilize algorithms that analyze user data, offering personalized insights and interventions. By leveraging machine learning and natural language processing, these apps can adapt to users' needs, providing timely support and fostering a sense of connection, even in the absence of traditional therapy.

One of the most notable features of successful AI mental health apps is their ability to offer real-time support. Users can engage with these applications anytime, anywhere, making mental health resources more accessible than ever. For instance, apps like Woebot and Wysa use conversational agents to interact with users, guiding them through cognitive behavioral therapy (CBT) techniques. This immediate access to mental health support can be particularly beneficial for individuals who may feel hesitant to seek help from a therapist or who live in areas with limited mental health resources.

Data privacy and user security are paramount when discussing AI-driven mental health solutions. Successful apps prioritize these aspects by employing robust encryption methods and transparency in data handling. Users are often required to grant consent before their data is used, and many apps provide clear information on how the data will be utilized. This commitment to user privacy fosters trust and encourages individuals to engage with the technology, knowing that their personal information is safeguarded.

Moreover, successful AI mental health apps often incorporate community features that enhance the user experience. By creating a sense of belonging, these platforms encourage users to share their experiences and support one another. For example, some apps include forums or group chats where users can connect, share coping strategies, and provide encouragement. This community aspect not only alleviates feelings of isolation but also enriches the effectiveness of the app by allowing users to learn from one another.

Finally, ongoing research and development are crucial for the continued success of AI mental health apps. Developers must consistently evaluate the effectiveness of their algorithms and update them based on user feedback and the latest psychological research. This iterative process ensures that the apps remain relevant and effective in addressing the evolving needs of users. As technology advances, so too will the capabilities of these applications, paving the way for a future where AI plays a vital role in mental health care and wellbeing.

Integrating AI into Traditional Therapy

Integrating AI into traditional therapy represents a transformative shift in the mental health landscape, offering new tools and methodologies that can enhance therapeutic practices. Traditional therapy, rooted in human interaction and the nuances of interpersonal relationships, has long been the cornerstone of mental health treatment. However, the advent of artificial intelligence introduces innovative approaches that can complement and enrich these traditional methods. By leveraging data-driven insights, AI can help therapists tailor their interventions to better meet the unique needs of each individual, thus fostering a more personalized therapeutic experience.

One of the most significant benefits of incorporating AI into traditional therapy is the ability to analyze vast amounts of data quickly and accurately. AI algorithms can process information from multiple sources, including patient histories, treatment responses, and even biometric data collected through wearable devices. This analysis enables therapists to identify patterns and trends that may not be readily apparent through conventional methods. For instance, predictive analytics can highlight potential relapses or shifts in a patient's mental health status, allowing therapists to intervene proactively. This data-driven approach empowers therapists to make informed decisions and adapt treatment plans in real-time, enhancing overall effectiveness.

Moreover, AI can serve as a valuable adjunct to the human elements of therapy. Virtual mental health assistants, powered by AI, can provide support between sessions, helping patients manage their symptoms and stay engaged with their treatment plans. These tools can offer immediate coping strategies, mindfulness exercises, or even just a friendly reminder to practice self-care. By maintaining a continuous line of communication, AI can help bridge the gaps between sessions, ensuring that patients feel supported throughout their journey. This ongoing engagement can reinforce the therapeutic alliance and contribute to better outcomes over time.

In addition to enhancing individual therapy, AI can facilitate group therapy sessions and community support systems. AI-driven platforms can analyze group dynamics, monitor interactions, and provide insights into the collective emotional state of participants. This capability allows therapists to tailor group activities and discussions to better address the needs of the group as a whole. Furthermore, AI can help identify individuals who may be struggling within a group context, ensuring that no one feels isolated or overlooked. By fostering a more collaborative environment, AI can enhance the therapeutic experience for all participants.

However, the integration of AI into traditional therapy is not without challenges. Ethical considerations, such as data privacy and the potential for algorithmic bias, must be addressed to ensure that these technologies are used responsibly and equitably. Therapists need to be aware of the limitations of AI, recognizing that it should complement, rather than replace, the human connection that is vital to effective therapy. By approaching the integration of AI with caution and mindfulness, practitioners can harness its potential while maintaining the core values of empathy and understanding that define traditional therapy. Through thoughtful collaboration between technology and human insight, the future of mental health treatment can become more effective, accessible, and responsive to the needs of individuals.

Lessons Learned from AI Implementations

The integration of artificial intelligence into mental health solutions has unfolded a myriad of lessons that can inform future implementations. First and foremost, the importance of data quality cannot be overstated. AI algorithms thrive on data, and the effectiveness of these systems is directly tied to the quality of the input they receive. Inadequate or biased data can lead to skewed results, which may compromise the efficacy of mental health interventions. Thus, practitioners and developers must prioritize sourcing high-quality, diverse datasets to ensure that AI-driven tools are both accurate and representative of the population they serve.

Another critical lesson is the need for interdisciplinary collaboration. The intersection of technology and mental health requires input from psychologists, data scientists, and ethicists alike. Each of these perspectives contributes vital insights that can enhance the development and deployment of AI systems. For instance, psychologists can guide the algorithms in understanding human emotions and behaviors, while ethicists can help navigate the moral implications of AI in sensitive areas such as mental health. This collaborative approach not only enriches the development process but also fosters a culture of accountability and trust among stakeholders.

User engagement is also a pivotal aspect of successful AI implementations in mental health. Feedback from end-users—whether they are mental health professionals or patients—provides invaluable insights into the usability and effectiveness of AI tools. Understanding user experiences can help refine algorithms and improve overall functionality. Moreover, involving users in the design process can enhance the acceptance and integration of these technologies into existing mental health practices. This user-centric approach ensures that AI solutions are tailored to actual needs rather than theoretical assumptions.

Ethical considerations are paramount in the realm of AI-driven mental health solutions. The deployment of AI technologies raises significant questions about privacy, consent, and the potential for misuse of sensitive data. It is essential for organizations to establish robust ethical frameworks that prioritize patient confidentiality and informed consent. Transparency about how data is collected, used, and protected fosters trust and encourages users to engage with AI tools without fear of exploitation. Furthermore, ongoing discussions about ethical guidelines can help shape policy and regulatory measures that govern AI in mental health.

Finally, the importance of continuous evaluation and adaptation cannot be overlooked. The landscape of mental health care is dynamic, and as new challenges arise, AI systems must evolve to meet these demands. Regular assessment of AI implementations allows for the identification of areas needing improvement, ensuring that interventions remain relevant and effective. By embracing a culture of learning and adaptation, organizations can harness the full potential of AI while remaining responsive to the needs of individuals seeking mental health support. This commitment to ongoing improvement ultimately leads to better outcomes and a more resilient mental health care system.

Chapter 7:

The Future of **AI** in Mental Health

Emerging Technologies and Trends

Emerging technologies are reshaping various sectors, and mental health care is no exception. The integration of artificial intelligence (AI) into mental health solutions is revolutionizing how practitioners approach diagnosis, treatment, and patient engagement. AI-driven algorithms are increasingly capable of analyzing vast amounts of data, identifying patterns, and providing insights that can lead to more personalized treatment plans. As these technologies advance, they hold the potential to enhance the efficacy of mental health interventions, making them more accessible and tailored to individual needs.

One of the most significant trends in this domain is the rise of digital therapeutics. These evidence-based interventions leverage software to prevent, manage, or treat mental health conditions. Digital therapeutics can include mobile applications, virtual reality experiences, and online counseling platforms. By offering convenient and scalable solutions, these tools can help bridge the gap between traditional therapy and the increasing demand for mental health services. Their ability to provide real-time feedback and track user progress can empower individuals to take an active role in their mental health journey.

Machine learning algorithms are also playing a crucial role in enhancing mental health diagnostics. By analyzing data from various sources, including social media activity, wearable devices, and self-reported mood logs, AI can help identify early signs of mental health issues. This proactive approach allows for timely interventions that can prevent conditions from worsening. Furthermore, these algorithms can continue to learn and adapt over time, improving their accuracy and effectiveness in predicting mental health trends and outcomes.

Another emerging trend is the use of chatbots and virtual assistants in mental health support. These AI-driven tools can provide immediate, round-the-clock assistance, offering users a sense of companionship and support when human therapists may not be available. While they cannot replace traditional therapy, chatbots can serve as a valuable supplement, offering coping strategies and resources for individuals experiencing mild to moderate mental health challenges. Their ability to engage users in a conversational manner can help reduce stigma and encourage individuals to seek help.

As we look to the future, it is essential to consider the ethical implications of these emerging technologies. Issues such as data privacy, consent, and the potential for algorithmic bias must be addressed to ensure that AI-driven mental health solutions are both effective and equitable. By fostering an open dialogue among stakeholders, including mental health professionals, technologists, and patients, we can create a framework that prioritizes ethical standards while harnessing the potential of AI for improved mental health outcomes. Embracing these technologies responsibly can lead to a more inclusive and effective mental health care system, ultimately benefiting society as a whole.

The Role of Human-AI Collaboration

The integration of artificial intelligence into mental health care represents a significant paradigm shift, emphasizing the importance of human-AI collaboration. This collaboration is not about replacing human professionals but enhancing their capabilities and improving patient outcomes. By leveraging AI's analytical power, mental health providers can gain insights that were previously unattainable. For example, AI algorithms can analyze vast amounts of data from diverse sources, identifying patterns and trends that may inform treatment plans more effectively than traditional methods. This partnership allows clinicians to focus on the human aspects of care while AI handles the data-heavy lifting.

AI-driven tools have the potential to support clinicians in diagnosing mental health conditions. By utilizing natural language processing and machine learning, AI systems can analyze patient interactions, identifying key indicators of mental health issues that may not be immediately evident to human practitioners. This capability enables a more accurate and timely diagnosis, which is particularly important in mental health, where early intervention can lead to significantly better outcomes. Furthermore, AI can assist in tracking patient progress over time, providing clinicians with ongoing data that can enhance their understanding of individual patient needs.

Human-AI collaboration also fosters a more personalized approach to mental health treatment. AI systems can analyze an individual's unique data, including genetic, behavioral, and environmental factors, to tailor interventions that best suit their needs. This individualized approach stands in contrast to one-size-fits-all solutions, promoting a more nuanced understanding of mental health. For instance, algorithm-driven recommendations for therapy types, medication options, or lifestyle changes can be made based on a comprehensive analysis of the patient's profile, leading to more effective and targeted treatment strategies.

Moreover, the role of human intuition and empathy cannot be overstated in this collaboration. While AI can process data and identify trends, it lacks the emotional intelligence that human therapists possess. The therapeutic relationship relies heavily on empathy, trust, and understanding, which are essential for effective treatment. Thus, the optimal use of AI in mental health care is as an augmentative tool that supports, rather than replaces, the human touch. Clinicians equipped with AI insights can enhance their interactions with patients, leading to more meaningful and productive therapy sessions.

Finally, as we embrace AI in mental health care, it is crucial to address ethical considerations and ensure that these technologies are used responsibly. Transparency in AI algorithms, safeguarding patient data, and maintaining a focus on patient well-being are essential components of this collaboration. As we navigate the complexities of mental health treatment in conjunction with AI advancements, fostering a partnership that upholds ethical standards will ensure that both human and machine work together toward a common goal: improved mental health outcomes for all individuals. This collaboration promises a future where mental health care is more effective, accessible, and personalized, ultimately benefiting society as a whole.

Preparing for the Next Generation of Mental Health Solutions

Preparing for the next generation of mental health solutions requires a comprehensive understanding of both current challenges and the potential of emerging technologies. As mental health concerns continue to rise globally, traditional methods of treatment often fall short in accessibility, efficacy, and personalization. The integration of artificial intelligence into mental health care presents a unique opportunity to address these issues. By leveraging AI-driven solutions, practitioners can enhance patient outcomes and create a more responsive and tailored approach to mental wellness.

The first step in preparing for AI-driven mental health solutions involves educating stakeholders about the technology's capabilities and limitations. Mental health professionals, patients, and policymakers must engage in discussions about how AI can augment traditional therapeutic techniques. This includes understanding how algorithms can analyze vast amounts of data to identify patterns in behavior and mood, leading to more accurate diagnoses and personalized treatment plans. Addressing misconceptions about AI is crucial; it should be seen as a tool to assist rather than replace human empathy and insight in therapy.

Next, the development of ethically sound frameworks for implementing AI in mental health care is paramount. Issues of privacy, data security, and informed consent must be prioritized to ensure that patients feel safe and respected when engaging with these technologies. Professionals in the field must collaborate with ethicists and technologists to establish guidelines that uphold patient rights and promote transparency. This collaborative approach will foster trust among users and help mitigate fears surrounding AI's role in sensitive areas like mental health.

Moreover, fostering innovation in AI-driven mental health solutions requires a commitment to continuous research and development. Mental health professionals and technologists should work together to explore new algorithms that can enhance therapeutic outcomes. This includes utilizing machine learning to refine treatment recommendations based on real-time data and patient feedback. Investment in training programs for mental health practitioners will also be crucial, equipping them with the skills needed to interpret AI-generated insights and integrate them into their practice effectively.

Finally, engaging patients in the development and implementation process ensures that solutions are user-centric and meet real-world needs. Feedback from individuals utilizing these new technologies can guide improvements and help shape future innovations. Creating platforms for patient participation fosters a sense of ownership and community, empowering users to contribute to their mental health journey. By prioritizing collaboration, ethics, and continuous improvement, we can prepare for a future where AI-driven mental health solutions not only complement traditional therapies but revolutionize the way we approach mental wellness.

Chapter 8:

Practical Steps for Embracing AI in Mental Health

Finding the Right Tools for You

Finding the right tools for your mental health journey can be a transformative experience, especially in a landscape increasingly shaped by technology. With the rise of AI-driven mental health solutions, individuals are presented with a variety of resources that can cater to their unique needs. Understanding the array of options available is crucial for effectively leveraging these tools. Each individual's mental health journey is distinct, and what works for one person may not resonate with another. Therefore, taking the time to explore and assess the tools that align with your specific preferences and requirements is essential.

Start by identifying your primary mental health needs. Are you seeking support for anxiety, depression, or stress management? Or perhaps you are looking for tools that enhance your overall well-being and resilience. By clarifying your goals, you can filter the vast array of AI-driven solutions. Many platforms offer assessments to help you pinpoint your needs, which can serve as a helpful starting point. This initial step is vital, as it can guide you toward tools specifically designed to address your concerns, thereby increasing the likelihood of a positive experience.

Once you have identified your needs, explore the different types of tools available. AI-driven mental health applications range from chatbots that provide immediate support to platforms that offer guided therapy sessions. Additionally, there are tools that facilitate journaling, mindfulness, and meditation, each employing algorithms to personalize the experience based on user interactions. Researching these options can provide insight into their functionalities and the underlying technology, helping you make informed decisions. Look for user reviews and testimonials, as these can offer valuable perspectives on the effectiveness of various tools.

Another crucial factor in finding the right tools is considering the user interface and overall experience. A tool's design can significantly impact your engagement and motivation to utilize it regularly. Some applications are user-friendly and visually appealing, while others may feel cumbersome or overwhelming. It's important to select tools that not only meet your mental health needs but also resonate with your personal preferences. Take advantage of free trials or demos whenever possible, allowing you to interact with the tools before committing to them fully.

Finally, remember that your mental health journey is an ongoing process, and finding the right tools may require some trial and error. As you experiment with different AI-driven solutions, remain open to adjusting your approach based on your experiences. The landscape of mental health technology is continually evolving, with new tools and features emerging regularly. Staying informed about advancements in AI and mental health can further enrich your toolkit. Ultimately, the goal is to cultivate a personalized approach to mental well-being that empowers you to embrace the potential of technology while prioritizing your mental health needs.

Building a Supportive Environment

Creating a supportive environment is crucial in the context of mental health, particularly when integrating AI-driven solutions. A supportive environment fosters trust, openness, and a sense of belonging, which are essential for individuals to engage fully with AI tools designed to enhance their mental well-being. This environment can be established both in physical spaces and in virtual interactions, ensuring that individuals feel comfortable sharing their thoughts and emotions. It is important to remember that mental health is not solely a personal journey; it is also a collective experience that can benefit from communal support.

One of the foundational elements of a supportive environment is the presence of empathy and understanding among peers and professionals. When individuals feel that their experiences are validated, they are more likely to open up about their mental health challenges. AI-driven mental health solutions can play a significant role in this by providing personalized insights and recommendations that resonate with individuals' unique experiences. By ensuring that these technologies are designed with empathy in mind, developers can create tools that not only analyze data but also communicate in a compassionate manner, enhancing the overall user experience.

In addition to fostering empathy, education is a key component of building a supportive environment. Individuals must be informed about how AI technologies work, what data they collect, and how they can be used to improve mental health outcomes. Distributing clear and accessible information can demystify AI tools and alleviate concerns about privacy and efficacy. Workshops, webinars, and informational resources can empower users to take an active role in their mental health journey, ensuring they understand the benefits and limitations of AI-driven solutions. This educational component helps cultivate an informed community that can support one another in navigating the complexities of mental health.

Furthermore, creating a feedback loop between users and developers is essential for refining AI-driven mental health tools. Encouraging individuals to share their experiences with these technologies can lead to iterative improvements that enhance their effectiveness. This collaborative approach not only builds trust but also fosters a sense of ownership among users. When individuals see that their feedback is valued and leads to tangible changes, they are more likely to engage deeply with AI solutions. This participatory model can further strengthen the supportive environment, as users feel they are contributing to the development of tools that serve their needs.

Lastly, inclusivity should be at the forefront of building a supportive environment for mental health. AI-driven solutions must cater to diverse populations, recognizing the varied backgrounds, cultures, and experiences of individuals. By designing systems that are adaptable and sensitive to different needs, developers can ensure that all individuals feel represented and supported. Initiatives aimed at increasing accessibility, such as language options and culturally relevant content, can enhance user engagement and satisfaction. A truly supportive environment is one where everyone feels acknowledged and has the opportunity to thrive, regardless of their circumstances.

Staying Informed and Engaged

Staying informed and engaged is crucial for anyone navigating the rapidly evolving landscape of mental health, particularly as it intersects with technology. The advent of AI-driven solutions has transformed how individuals access mental health resources, enabling a more personalized approach to emotional well-being. Understanding these advancements allows consumers to make informed decisions about their mental health care and to recognize the tools available for self-improvement. Knowledge empowers individuals to discern between various applications and platforms, ensuring they choose those that align with their unique needs and preferences.

One effective way to stay informed is by following reputable sources that specialize in mental health and technology. Academic journals, professional organizations, and trusted mental health websites provide valuable insights into the latest research and trends in AI applications for mental health. Engaging with these sources not only enhances one's understanding of algorithmic solutions but also highlights their potential benefits and limitations. Furthermore, participating in webinars, workshops, and online forums focused on AI in mental health can foster a sense of community among those who share similar interests and concerns.

In addition to consuming information, individuals can actively engage with the technology that supports their mental health. This means exploring various AI-driven applications designed for self-care, therapy, or stress management. By experimenting with different platforms, individuals can find tools that resonate with them personally, whether through guided meditation apps, chatbots for immediate support, or platforms that connect users with licensed therapists. Engagement is not just about usage; it's about developing a critical understanding of how these tools work and their underlying algorithms, which can empower users to advocate for better services and features.

Moreover, staying engaged with developments in AI and mental health can lead to participation in advocacy efforts. As the conversation around mental health and technology evolves, individuals can lend their voices to discussions about ethics, accessibility, and the effectiveness of AI-driven solutions. Advocacy can take many forms, from sharing personal experiences and insights on social media to participating in policy discussions that shape the future of mental health care. By becoming active participants in this dialogue, individuals can contribute to a more equitable and informed approach to mental health solutions.

Lastly, fostering a mindset of lifelong learning is essential in the context of algorithmic healing. Mental health is a dynamic field, and as new technologies emerge, so too do new challenges and opportunities. By committing to ongoing education—whether through formal courses, self-directed learning, or community engagement—individuals can ensure they remain equipped to navigate the complexities of AI in mental health. This proactive stance not only enhances personal mental health management but also cultivates a more informed society that values the intersection of technology and well-being.

Chapter 9:

Conclusion: Embracing Algorithmic Healing

Reflecting on the Journey

Reflecting on the journey of integrating artificial intelligence into mental health care reveals a landscape filled with transformative potential and significant challenges. As we have explored throughout this book, the algorithmic approach to mental health represents a paradigm shift in how we understand and manage emotional well-being. From personalized therapy recommendations to predictive analytics that identify at-risk individuals, AI-driven solutions have the capacity to enhance the therapeutic process significantly. This chapter invites readers to consider the milestones achieved and the ongoing evolution of mental health practices influenced by technology.

Throughout this journey, we have witnessed remarkable advancements in the field of AI. The development of sophisticated algorithms capable of analyzing vast datasets has allowed for the identification of patterns in human behavior that were previously inaccessible. By harnessing these insights, mental health professionals can tailor interventions to meet the specific needs of individuals. This personalized approach not only fosters a deeper understanding of the self but also encourages a sense of agency among patients, empowering them to take charge of their mental health journeys.

However, the integration of AI into mental health care is not without its ethical dilemmas and concerns. As we reflect on this journey, it is crucial to address the potential biases inherent in algorithmic design and data collection. The algorithms that power these mental health solutions must be carefully scrutinized to ensure they reflect diverse populations and experiences. An equitable approach to mental health care necessitates that we remain vigilant about the implications of these technologies and strive to create systems that prioritize inclusivity and fairness.

As we move forward, it is essential to cultivate a collaborative relationship between technology and human empathy. While AI can enhance the efficiency and effectiveness of mental health interventions, it cannot replace the human connection that is vital to the healing process. Mental health practitioners are encouraged to embrace AI tools as complementary resources that augment their therapeutic skills rather than as replacements. This synergy between technology and human insight will ultimately lead to more comprehensive care, enabling individuals to navigate their mental health challenges with greater resilience.

In conclusion, reflecting on the journey of algorithmic healing encourages us to celebrate our achievements while acknowledging the road ahead. As we continue to explore the intersection of AI and mental health, it is imperative that we foster an environment of ongoing learning, ethical consideration, and compassionate care. By embracing the potential of AI-driven mental health solutions, we can collectively work towards a future where mental health care is more accessible, personalized, and effective for all individuals, thereby enriching the human experience in profound ways.

The Importance of Continued Innovation

The importance of continued innovation in mental health care cannot be overstated, particularly in the context of algorithmic advancements and AI-driven solutions. As society becomes increasingly aware of mental health issues, the demand for effective and accessible treatment options rises. Traditional methods, while valuable, often fall short in addressing the diverse needs of individuals. Continued innovation in technology and algorithms offers new pathways for personalized care, enabling mental health solutions that can adapt to the unique circumstances of each individual.

One significant advantage of ongoing innovation is the ability to harness vast amounts of data to inform treatment strategies. AI algorithms can analyze patterns in behavior, mood, and other relevant metrics, allowing for more tailored interventions. This data-driven approach not only enhances understanding of individual experiences but also informs therapists and practitioners about the most effective methods for intervention. By leveraging real-time analytics, mental health solutions can evolve and improve continuously, which is essential in a field where individual needs can change rapidly.

Furthermore, continued innovation fosters collaboration among researchers, mental health professionals, and technology developers. This interdisciplinary approach accelerates the development of cutting-edge tools that integrate the latest findings in psychology with advanced algorithmic techniques. For example, AI-driven applications can be designed to deliver cognitive behavioral therapy in real-time, allowing users to engage with therapeutic techniques as challenges arise. This level of responsiveness can significantly enhance the effectiveness of treatment, making mental health resources more accessible and adaptable.

Moreover, as new technologies emerge, there is an opportunity to address existing barriers to mental health care. Geographical limitations, stigma, and lack of resources often hinder access to traditional mental health services. Innovative solutions, such as teletherapy and AI-based chatbots, can provide support to those who might otherwise go without help. By embracing these advancements, society can work towards a more inclusive mental health landscape, ensuring that support is available to everyone, regardless of their circumstances.

In conclusion, the importance of continued innovation in mental health care lies in its potential to transform the landscape of treatment and support. As algorithms and AI-driven solutions evolve, so too does the capacity to deliver personalized, effective care to individuals. Embracing these innovations not only enhances the quality of mental health services but also contributes to a broader understanding of mental well-being in our increasingly complex world. It is imperative that stakeholders in mental health continue to prioritize and invest in innovative approaches to ensure the future of mental health care is both accessible and effective for all.

A Vision for Holistic Mental Health Care

A vision for holistic mental health care involves integrating various aspects of an individual's life to foster overall well-being. In the context of advancing technology, particularly artificial intelligence, this vision becomes increasingly attainable. Holistic mental health care recognizes that mental health is not an isolated aspect of an individual's existence but rather interconnected with physical health, social relationships, and environmental factors. By embracing AI-driven solutions, we can create a more comprehensive approach that addresses the multifaceted nature of mental health.

AI has the potential to personalize mental health care in unprecedented ways. Traditional mental health treatments often follow a one-size-fits-all model, which may not consider the unique circumstances and needs of each individual. Algorithmic approaches can analyze vast amounts of data to identify patterns and correlations that inform personalized treatment plans. This data-driven insight can help practitioners tailor interventions based on an individual's specific situation, preferences, and responses, ultimately leading to more effective outcomes.

Moreover, the integration of AI into mental health care can enhance accessibility, allowing individuals to receive support when and where they need it. Telehealth solutions powered by AI can provide immediate assistance, reducing the barriers related to time, location, and stigma that often prevent people from seeking help. These platforms can facilitate ongoing monitoring and support through chatbots and virtual therapists, ensuring that individuals have access to resources and guidance 24/7. This level of accessibility is crucial for creating a supportive environment that encourages individuals to prioritize their mental health.

Collaboration between AI technology and mental health professionals is essential for realizing this vision. While AI can provide valuable insights and tools, the human element remains irreplaceable. Mental health practitioners play a critical role in interpreting data, understanding emotional nuances, and fostering therapeutic relationships. By combining the analytical power of AI with the empathy and expertise of mental health professionals, we can build a system that not only addresses symptoms but also empowers individuals to achieve long-term mental well-being.

Ultimately, a vision for holistic mental health care that incorporates AI-driven solutions paves the way for a more compassionate and effective approach to mental health. By recognizing the interconnectedness of mental, physical, and social health, we can create a system that fosters resilience and healing. As we move forward, it is crucial to prioritize ethical considerations, ensuring that AI is used responsibly and equitably. This vision invites us to embrace innovation while remaining grounded in the core values of empathy, respect, and understanding in our quest for better mental health outcomes for all.

A Blessing for the Reader

May this book be a gentle companion on your
journey—
a guide through the intersections of mind and
machine,
offering clarity where there is confusion,
and hope where there is struggle.

May you approach these pages with curiosity,
and leave with a deeper sense of compassion—
for yourself, for others,
and for the evolving tools that seek to serve our
healing.

May you find in these words not just information,
but inspiration—
to question boldly, to care deeply,
and to imagine a future where technology and
humanity walk hand in hand
toward wholeness.

And above all,
may your mind finds peace,
your heart finds courage,
and your path forward be guided by wisdom—
algorithmic or otherwise.

Krishna Dubey

Other books written by the same author:

1. Beyond the Self - Exploring Identity and Human Experience
2. Eco-Modern - Living Sustainably in Today's World
3. E-Commerce – Unlocking Digital Success in the Modern Marketplace
4. Family First – Mentorship Strategies for Young Achievers
5. Family Joy – Creating Lasting Happiness Together
6. Fearless Living - Cultivating Confidence in Everyday Life
7. Financial Freedom Formula - Steps to a Prosperous Life
8. Focus and Flourish - Learning Strategies for Academic Excellence
9. From Darkness to Dawn – A Journey Through Life Transformations
10. From Idea to Bestseller Your Step-by-Step Writing Guide
11. From Manager to Leader - Coaching Paths for Corporate Advancement
12. From Struggle to Strength – Embracing Your Inner Power
13. How to Clean Our Dirty Thoughts
14. Illuminating Paths – How Your Journey Inspires Others
15. Master Your Money Mindset – A Guide to Financial Freedom
16. Rich Soul – A Spiritual Guide to Healing Your Inner World
17. Soul Strong – A Spiritual Guide to Healing Your Inner World